BRUSH MIND:

SECOND HAND

2

HANK LAZER

for Mar de Jade

& for Laura

& for the ocean sounds

wisdom

water

a life's

work

it

goes

to

show

you

when   we

sit

together

el

vacío

wave

after

wave

seres

humanos

in this
we have
a lot
in common

your happiness

is

your

responsibility

rings

a

bell

you & i

do not know

what's

next

this consciousness

was

never

your own

we have been

placed

on notice

practice

gratitude

it's

up

to

you

awaken

to

joy

because

you are

here

no one else

can

die

in your place

su sabiduría

tan profundo

como

el mar

as

you

wish

hugh said
his brother
became uppity
when he put on
the badge

i

don't know

what

to say

it's all

a

conversation

the apparition

of

damn near

anything

todos los seres

en

todos los mundos

do

be

taken

in

sweet

to be here

with you

now

give

thanks

to   your

eyes

she
made it
possible
for you

prometo

entrar

awake

this consciousness

was

here

before you

i think
i see
what
you mean

what about

five

minutes

from

now

felt

presence

think

what

you're

missing

how

would

i

know

it's

possible

jim's   eyes

lit up

talking about

that pristine lake

scriabin

etudes

who

knew

stretching

well

before

dawn

practice

direct
awareness
to your
heart

exactly

as

exactly

for a moment
right now
stop
thinking

many small

mushrooms

arise

after the rain

walk

slowly

listen

carefully

where

are

you

now

i

am

trying

to reach you

flip

turn

what

you are

becoming

light

moving

through

your eyes

do not wish
to be
other
than you are

sudden

joy

whenever

you

are

ready

no
preparation
required
just begin
to
pay attention

the day

is

for

giving

under

one

roof

this

is

what

we are

given

play

along

dust

ashes

light

sit

for pleasure

slowing

time

we are

in this

together

www.ingramcontent.com/pod-product-compliance
Lightning Source LLC
Chambersburg PA
CBHW080516030726
47592CB00012B/3369